Intuition of a Leader

Intuition of a Leader

Roberta J. Goheen

Energy
Drive
Inspiration
And Motivation
Towards The Vision

First Printing: 2012
Revised: 2016

ISBN ISBN 978-1-4583-5338-2

Synthesis Management Group
www.getsynthesis.com

What You Will Find In This Book

Acknowledgements

I would like to thank Kathy Palokoff who edited this book and brought it to a level I could not have done on my own. Kathy's ability to understand the vision and close the gaps I had missed makes this a better experience for you.

I would like to thank those who believe in me everyday and in everyway... My husband, Matthew, and sons Rigel and Cal. Finally, this would not come into being without the constant hum of my tribe Donald, Anita, Donita, David, Diane, Annika, Dan, David F., JR, Emma, Haley, Drew, Derek, Bryan, Mac, Martha, Jon, Lysa, Suzy, Pat, Bridget, Cindy, Lisa, Kathie, Amy, Laurie, Lau-reen, Karen, Dawn, Anne, Dawn, Denise, Leslie, Lorraine, Mona, Pam, Sue, Trish, Amy, Moira, Joyce, Gretchen, Joyce, Nicole, Cathy, Christine, Gayle, Josanne, Sally, Tracy, Christy, Myrna, Ellie, Mindy, Kathy, Ann, Barbara, Leanne, Marcia, Joan, Anne, Annie, Andrea, Barb, Bear, Chandra, Ginny, Jalaja, Miki, Kelly, Adam, Patrick, Don, Ralph, Rich, RAD, and Tony

Introduction

Following Our Intuition

"Our gift, our strength, and our path is our intuition.

The ability to know your inner voice, follow it, and live by it creates unparallel satisfaction, fulfillment and success.

Every fabulous leader I know has developed the ability to get quiet to listen and follow.

This is part of our heritage and there is no school for it.

We stumble upon it after we are tired of stumbling in life.

You have to have the courage to claim your inner voice and follow it...for it knows the best path for you.

It has never steered me wrong."

Roberta "Bobbie" Goheen

*"What lies behind us
and what lies before us are tiny matters
compared to what lies within us."*
--Ralph Waldo Emerson

Putting a Ding in the Universe

Why

"I want to put a ding in the universe."
-- Steve Jobs, Inventor and Marketing Guy

After coaching and developing leaders for nearly 30 years, I have seen how leaders thrive. The leaders who thrive -- put a ding in the universe – believe in the concepts outlined in this book.

Some seem to intuitively trust the concepts and move with swiftness. Others need to wrestle and challenge them before they can move. And some leaders need to see others go first. No matter how you learn, if you are committed to positive growth you will move through these concepts.

In this first in the series of "pen to paper," I invite you to a unique conversation with the leader within to define the kinds of insights, awareness and actions that honor you and ultimately others.

The passion I have behind this series is to provide access to any individual who wants to live in their fullest sense of self. It comes from training over a thousand leaders throughout my career and being privileged to see what takes and what does not. And it is written from a deep understanding of the nature of our humanity.

My Story

Early on in my career, I was lucky to be working with a progressive, high growth Fortune 500 company. I managed and led a team of outstanding, compassionate, capable and creative people who built one of the first corporate universities and world class training programs. Our focus was how to get people up to speed quickly and create a path for short and long term success.

I encouraged the team to explore every avenue of learning from early childhood "learn through play" methods to Ivy League "stretch your critical thinking." We rocked when it came to technical, sales, service, management and leadership training. That experience led to new ways of learning, leading and, ultimately, coaching.

One of the insights I had was that learning becomes easy when people believe in themselves. This became the cornerstone of my business that I started over a decade ago.

In my decades of actively leading a team, birthing new ideas for myself or others, coaching leaders and facilitating lead teams, this is what I now know:

If you know what people believe and where they want to go, you can co-create a path which honors them and those around them.

To thrive as a leader takes the ability to have a dream, believe in it, understand your own nature of self, listen to your intuition, speak your truth with authenticity and inspiration, and make sure your actions are in alignment with your dream/vision. While this might seem trite and rather easy, it is not.

Many leaders do not take the time to listen to their intuition. Many have not been taught how to listen. That is why the first book in this series is called "Intuition of a Leader."

We are influenced by nature and often forget we are a part of it. We regularly cycle through:

- Spring -- new ideas

- Summer -- activation and cultivation of ideas

- Autumn -- the harvesting of ideas

- Winter -- the rest, becoming dormant, receiving, absorbing and quietness necessary so we can have a fresh spring

When we ignore these cycles of ourselves -- spending too much time doing (summer) without fresh thinking (spring) we don't have the same impact and become burnt out or worn out (no winter). When we try and control and limit change (spring), we have weak returns (autumn).

So learning how to live in, with and through the seasons of ourselves becomes more important to live life in a way where we are centered, satisfied, and fulfilled.

The people really make things happen in dynamic and inspiring ways are leaders who are path makers. Path makers learn from those around them. While they study what the best of the best have done or are doing, they always take the time to define a new path forward that is so compelling that others follow.

Leadership is not about copying or following. It is about finding a new path forward that attracts like individuals and compels them to listen, understand and move with you.

Life never really happens in the way we design it and yet what it has to offer is far better than we could have designed for ourselves.

Pen to Paper

One final word on why this is called the "The Pen to Paper Series." There is a power and shift that happens when we take the time to slow down and use our hands to write out our thinking.

The act of writing by hand connects and powers the right and left sides our brains. Additionally, studies have shown that the physical act of writing with a pen to paper boosts learning and goal achievement. There has been some research which shows writing stimulates cells at the base of the brain called the *reticular activating system (RAS)*. The RAS acts as a filter for everything your brain needs to process, giving more importance to the things that you're actively focusing on at the moment— something that the physical act of writing brings to the forefront. Writing triggers the RAS, which in turn sends a signal to the cerebral cortex: "Pay attention." Once you write down a goal, your brain is activated to achieve it, and will alert you to the signs and signals that were there all along.

While this data is new and evolving as technology shifts in our environment, it has been my personal experience and observation that the act of writing in the form of "pen to paper" settles the mind so the heart and voice of the individual comes out more clearly and with surprising insights.

At its essence, this ancient practice of writing helps us capture a pure and true glimpse of ourselves, our intuition, our truth and our path.

Learning a New Language of Leadership

LEADERSHIP

"You gain strength, courage, and confidence
by every experience
in which you really stop to look fear in the face.
You are able to say to yourself,
'I have lived through this horror.
I can take the next thing that comes along.'
You must do the thing you think you cannot do."
-- Eleanor Roosevelt, First Lady of United States 1933-1945

Leadership is about defining and crafting your own life. If you find yourself called to this book, you also will find yourself called to leadership. You claim this word as part of who you are in the world regardless if you have people working with you or not.

Leadership is the ability to claim:

- all who you are

- your voice

- your vision

- yourself with clarity, confidence and commitment

Many have found it difficult to step into their true sense of self as a leader based on:

- past definitions

- poor leadership experiences or examples

- a hesitancy to be bold enough to say one is a leader

As you step into the fullness of yourself, you step into your fullness as a leader. Not stepping creates a loss of momentum, a dullness to your creativity and a complacency that erodes your ability to participate and create in the world.

Here are a three important truths about leadership:

- Leaders are not born. They are made through the ongoing commitment of growth of the heart and mind.

- Leadership is not a position; it is a practice. To lead a life uncommon means a commitment to continual self-growth and evolution.

- Effective leadership happens when the individual comes from a place of authenticity and centeredness.

When you lead from your core, you move yourself and others forward. When people speak from the heart, they connect immediately to others.

VISION

"Your vision will become clear
only when you look into your heart ...
Who looks outside, dreams.
Who looks inside, awakens."
-- Carl Jung, Natural Scientist

To enter into the dance of leadership is a lifelong passion. Once you are aware of what it takes to live and thrive in this way, you will be unable to close the door on the possibilities and growth that happens as you deepen your practice.

Each one of us is born with the potential and greatness to be all of who we are in the world, expressing all we have within to the best of our ability and passion.

The dream and quest within us is to follow our joy, releasing it so that others may know and experience the gifts we have to offer. Conversely, as we equally join in experiencing and receiving the gifts of others, our own abilities, creativity and impact grow.

This doesn't sound too hard or too difficult. It is. We are raised with societal rules, etiquette and laws that provide structure to get where you want to go and do what needs to done to be good citizen.

But rules are merely the traffic lines on the road. To define your own roadmap, you must be willing to:

- Build it

- Work at it

- Craft it

- Walk it

By moving through this process of creating your own path and living a life uncommon, you will find satisfaction and fulfillment putting your hands on the steering wheel of your life.

Being the leader of your own life does not mean to bungee jump or sky dive. It means to have the guts to follow what is calling you from within. It means to clearly hear the message, understand it and know exactly what you are thinking with clarity and centeredness that say "yes" this is my true voice.

Having clear vision requires the following:

- Know your true voice.

- Take action in a way that honors your personal vision, mission and values.

- Flow. Take another action without trying to change, fix or improve it. See your vision and continue to move towards it.

INSTINCT

"Trust your own instinct.
Your mistakes might as well be your own,
instead of someone else's."
-- Billy Wilder, Film Artist

How many times have you wished you followed your instincts? The process of following your sense of things and seeing how things play out is what hones your strength of character and self.

You learn more about how to move into the unknown with confidence and curiosity. You remember you are a learner which puts you in a creative mode of moving forward. You will understand that mistakes will happen. You become comfortable that you will either figure out a way to work with it or can tap into someone who might know.

The fact of the matter is that you will fail whether you listen to someone else or not. Failure or making mistakes is the nature of life.

To think it will not happen to you is magical thinking. It happens to all of us. We all fall down. Those who are successful get back up quickly.

Openness, curiosity, and engagement are the assets that bring instincts to life and create wonderful possibilities.

Instinct is the crucial component in taking ordinary or stressful situations to extraordinary

In order to learn how to hone your instincts you have to let go of expectations and outcomes. This is the hardest lesson of all and one you may have to relearn many times. It is difficult because our society rewards us for achieving outcomes and meeting expectations.

As you build a portfolio of successes and achievements, you may forget the reason you achieve what you do is because of your instincts. You may begin to believe it is because of your knowledge and experience that you are successful.

This belief contains a small portion of the truth. The real truth is about:

- Going into situations

- Understanding what is happening

- Being truthful about what you do and don't know

- Working with and through others to define potential ways to move forward

- Beginning to move towards the vision

PASSION

"There is a vitality, a life force, an energy,
a quickening that is translated through you into action,
and because there is only one of you in all of time,
this expression is unique.
And if you block it,
it will never exist through any other medium
and it will be lost.
The world will not have it.
--Martha Graham, Pioneer of Modern Dance

Passion comes from our dreams, our vision. It is a right brained and heart activity and conversation. Once you provide regular space and activities for the right brain to live and thrive, you find yourself on fire with all you do.

Nothing good comes to life without unleashed and dynamic passion. This is the fuel that has you jump out of bed in the morning; the energy which makes you push good ideas through; and the tenacity to see things through. Those who allow passion to drive them find themselves on a fascinating journey.

Many people do not open this door because they want to be in control. They do not want to always be doing or changing. They are afraid of what unleashed passion could mean in their lives.

The truth is that passion is:

- Energy

- Drive

- Inspiration

- Motivation to move towards the dream/the vision

Without passion, we get ordinary or average results, which is not bad. But sometimes it feels that any result is better than none, yet we have a sense there is more...

If you feeling dull or listless, simply ask what does my passion want to create now? And then do it.

If you are edgy or restless, it is time to express the ideas you have within you. Do it.

If you are on fire with ideas and concepts, get them out, work with them, and follow them until they begin to match the concept inside your mind.

Don't worry about getting it right the first time. Worry about getting it out. Get it started. **NOW.**

VOICE

"When I have been most effective,
I have listened to my inner voice."
-- Norman Lear, Artist

The ability to speak your truth is the beginning of honing your voice. When you speak your truth, you connect to your heart and say things based on your sense, experience, insight, and awareness.

Understanding the analytical brain -- the left side -- is a strong and useful tool for calculating, organizing, planning and evaluating. But when we speak from the analytical brain, we lose the passion, heart and authentic voice that connects with people to have them tune into the concepts we wish to share.

All motivation and inspiration of meaningful change comes from leaders who are able to capture the heart of people. If you desire to move in this direction, tying into your heart, voice and truth brings forth a dynamic and authentic conversation that resonates for many.

If you do only one thing switch how you communicate by accessing the right side of the brain and let the left side follow to do clean up and plan it out.

INTUITION

"There are no rules.

Just follow your heart."

-- Robin Williams, Actor and Comedian

To create your own path requires the ability to listen to your voice, your intuition. Since as a society we have lost these teachings, it is not always innate within us.

As you develop the ability to listen to your voice, your intuition... you will feel uncertain, doubtful and sometimes fearful. The ability to follow your intuition is risk taking. The more you follow the more you are able to listen, heed and understand what to do next. This in itself represents risk for many people because they are use to following what others do instead of creating their own path.

Learning to listen to your voice builds confidence in:

- Who you are

- What you are thinking

- Recognizing that other's thoughts are their own, not yours.

In order to follow your intuition, you have to give up ownership of the idea that you can plan, plot and control everything.

To follow your intuition requires the ability to take risks because the path is not always clear when you are making it.

To be a risk taker, you have to know that you may not be going with the flow of well laid out plans of others. It is more important to flow with:

- Who you are

- Where you are called

- What is your nature

- How to get where you desire to go

Some choose not to develop the ability to listen to their intuition and to stay safe in their predictable roles of their life. That is exactly where they need to be for whom, how, and where they are in their lives, until they sense within themselves there is another way. This sense or inner knowing begins the journey of following the heart.

Your intuition is much like learning how to ride a bicycle. You will fall off many times until you find your balance. The key is when you fall off is to get back on the bike.

As you begin to excavate and pay attention to your intuition, you will experience indicators of "falling off your intuition." For example, after an event occurs you admit to yourself that you "had a feeling about this" or you just sensed "something was not quite right."

Take a few moments right now and sift through your memories when you said to yourself "I should have followed my instinct," or "my gut said this was wrong."

If you have had these moments, you are ready to begin the re-connection to your inner homing device -- intuition.

Applying and Activating Your Intuition

" Only those who risk going to far can possibly find out how far one can go. "

~T.S. Eliot

INTUITION EXCAVATION #1

"The only real valuable thing is intuition."

--Albert Einstein

Use the following guideline to excavate the moment and begin to understand your indicators for intuition:

Consider a defining moment when you knew you should have listened to your intuition.

_____

_____

_____

_____

_____

_____

_____

What happened?

_____

_____

_____

_____

_____

_____

_____

When you look back to your early indicators what did you sense?

_____

_____

_____

_____

_____

_____

_____

_____

_____

How did your body react to the situation?

_____

_____

_____

_____

_____

_____

_____

_____

_____

What were the behaviors that you exhibited?

_____

_____

_____

_____

_____

_____

_____

_____

_____

_____

_____

_____

What were the internal voices that told you to ignore your instincts?

_____

_____

_____

_____

_____

_____

_____

_____

_____

_____

_____

_____

_____

What felt wrong about the situation?

_____

_____

_____

_____

_____

_____

_____

_____

_____

_____

What felt right about the situation?

_____

_____

_____

_____

_____

_____

_____

_____

_____

_____

INTUITION EXCAVATION #2

*"The struggle....to learn to listen to and respect
(our) own intuitive, inner promptings is the greatest challenge
of all"*

-- Herb Goldberg

Think back to a moment that felt like a "golden moment" for you when everything just clicked. Describe it.

_____

_____

_____

_____

_____

_____

_____

What were the events or indicators that told you this was a good direction or choice to make?

_____

_____

_____

_____

_____

_____

_____

How did your body feel about the decision?

_____
_____
_____
_____
_____
_____
_____
_____
_____

Have you had similar moments in your lifetime?

_____
_____
_____
_____
_____
_____
_____
_____
_____
_____

Were there any additional indicators you would add to your list?

_____

_____

_____

_____

_____

_____

_____

_____

_____

_____

_____

What felt wrong about the situation?

_____

_____

_____

_____

_____

_____

_____

_____

_____

_____

_____

What felt right about the situation?

_____

_____

_____

_____

_____

_____

_____

_____

_____

_____

What did you not want to happen?

_____

_____

_____

_____

_____

_____

_____

_____

_____

_____

What did you want to happen?

_____

_____

_____

_____

_____

_____

_____

What internal beliefs supported your choice?

_____

_____

_____

_____

_____

_____

_____

What felt risky, if anything?

_____

_____

_____

_____

_____

_____

_____

"By saying yes
to your true nature,
you will be making a strong connection
to your highest values."
~Alexandra Stoddard

INTUITION INDICATORS

"Yes, risk taking is inherently failure-prone.
Otherwise, it would be called sure-thing-taking."
-- Tim McMahon

Review what you have discovered for indicators when things go well and didn't go well.

Complete the following to develop your indicators for choices that honor you.

What are the indicators that have worked well for you and the indicators you would definitely look for in the future?

_____

_____

_____

_____

_____

_____

_____

_____

_____

_____

_____

_____

_____

_____

_____

_____

_____

_____

_____

_____

_____

_____

_____

_____

_____

If you had to make a decision today that would change your life forever (take a job in a foreign country, start a high potential new venture with no working capital, take a six-month trek through the Amazon, etc.), do you feel that this list provides you with enough indicators to help you make the right decision for another "golden moment" with no regrets?

If yes, keep this list with you as you move through each day to support your daily life choices. Add as you find more positive indicators.

If no, what other indicators would be necessary for you to feel solid?

_____

_____

_____

_____

_____

_____

_____

_____

_____

_____

_____

_____

_____

Have you had an opportunity to test these indicators out in past situations?

_____

_____

_____

_____

_____

_____

_____

_____

_____

_____

If yes, what was the outcome?

_____

_____

_____

_____

_____

_____

_____

_____

_____

_____

If no, are there any current choices that you could test these indicators out without too much hardship to yourself?

_____
_____
_____
_____
_____
_____
_____
_____
_____
_____
_____
_____
_____
_____
_____
_____
_____
_____
_____
_____
_____
_____

*"The heart is the hub of all sacred places.
Go there and roam in it."*

~ Sri Nityananda

RISK TAKING EXCAVATION

"It is not because things are difficult that we do not dare,

it is because we do not dare that they are difficult."

-- Seneca

Now I would like you to take a moment and think about a time when you took a risk and it was the right choice for you.

What did you know about the decision you made?

_____

_____

_____

_____

_____

_____

_____

_____

_____

_____

_____

_____

_____

_____

_____

_____

Why did it feel right to you?

_____

_____

_____

_____

_____

_____

_____

_____

_____

_____

Why does this moment stand out for you?

_____

_____

_____

_____

_____

_____

_____

_____

_____

_____

_____

_____

How did you body feel when you made the choice to take this risk?

_____

_____

_____

_____

_____

_____

_____

_____

_____

_____

_____

What did you sense?

_____

_____

_____

_____

_____

_____

_____

_____

_____

_____

_____

What were the behaviors that you exhibited?

_____

_____

_____

_____

_____

_____

_____

_____

_____

_____

_____

What made it a risk for you?

_____

_____

_____

_____

_____

_____

_____

_____

_____

_____

_____

INSIGHT JOURNAL

"Listen to your own Self.
If you listen within,
then you find the Truth."
-- Kabir

Every day learn to make decisions and choices from your intuition and continue to hone in on what feels right about a choice and what feels off regardless of outcome.

Journal your intuition insights for seven days on the following pages.

"Trust yourself you know more than you think you do. Trust in your abilities, your strengths, your values and your intuition – you know much more than you give yourself credit for."

~ Unknown

DAY 1

"I go by instinct.... I don't worry about experience."

-- Barbra Streisand

List briefly the decisions and choices you made from your intuition:

_____

_____

_____

_____

_____

_____

_____

_____

_____

_____

_____

_____

_____

_____

_____

_____

_____

_____

_____

_____

_____

_____

_____

_____

How did it feel to make the choices/decisions from intuition?

_____

_____

_____

_____

_____

_____

_____

_____

_____

_____

_____

_____

_____

_____

_____

_____

_____

_____

_____

_____

_____

_____

_____

_____

What new insights or concepts will you take forward into the next day based on your experiences?

_____

_____

_____

_____

_____

_____

_____

_____

_____

_____

_____

_____

List three reasons or items why you are grateful for your intuition today:

_____

_____

_____

_____

_____

_____

_____

_____

Day 2

"One of the reasons so few of us act vs. react, is because we are continually stifling our deepest impulses."

-- Henry Miller

List briefly the decisions and choices you made from your intuition:

_____

_____

_____

_____

_____

_____

_____

_____

_____

_____

_____

_____

_____

_____

_____

_____

_____

_____

_____

_____

_____

_____

_____

_____

_____

How did it feel to make the choices/decisions from intuition?

_____

_____

_____

_____

_____

_____

_____

_____

_____

_____

_____

_____

_____

_____

_____

_____

_____

_____

_____

_____

_____

_____

_____

_____

_____

_____

_____

What new insights or concepts will you take forward into the next day based on your experiences?

_____

_____

_____

_____

_____

_____

_____

_____

_____

_____

List three reasons or items why you are grateful for your intuition today:

_____

_____

_____

_____

_____

_____

_____

_____

_____

_____

Day 3

"Every time I've done something that does not feel right, it's ended up not being right."

-- Mario Cuomo

List briefly the decisions and choices you made from your intuition:

_____

_____

_____

_____

_____

_____

_____

_____

_____

_____

_____

_____

_____

_____

_____

_____

_____

_____

_____

_____

_____

_____

_____

How did it feel to make the choices/decisions from intuition?

What new insights or concepts will you take forward into the next day based on your experiences?

_____

_____

_____

_____

_____

_____

_____

_____

_____

_____

List three reasons or items why you are grateful for your intuition today:

_____

_____

_____

_____

_____

_____

_____

_____

_____

_____

_____

Day 4

"Belief consists in accepting the affirmations of the soul; unbelief in denying them."

-- Ralph Waldo Emerson

List briefly the decisions and choices you made from your intuition:

_____

_____

_____

_____

_____

_____

_____

_____

_____

_____

_____

_____

_____

_____

_____

_____

_____

_____

_____

_____

_____

_____

_____

How did it feel to make the choices/decisions from intuition?

_____

_____

_____

_____

_____

_____

_____

_____

_____

_____

_____

_____

_____

_____

_____

_____

_____

_____

_____

_____

_____

_____

_____

_____

_____

_____

_____

What new insights or concepts will you take forward into the next day based on your experiences?

_____

_____

_____

_____

_____

_____

_____

_____

_____

_____

List three reasons or items why you are grateful for your intuition today:

_____

_____

_____

_____

_____

_____

_____

_____

_____

_____

Day 5

"Intuition is a spiritual faculty and does not explain, but simply points the way."

-- Florence Scovel Shinn

List briefly the decisions and choices you made from your intuition:

_____

_____

_____

_____

_____

_____

_____

_____

_____

_____

_____

_____

_____

_____

_____

_____

_____

_____

_____

_____

_____

_____

How did it feel to make the choices/decisions from intuition?

What new insights or concepts will you take forward into the next day based on your experiences?

_____

_____

_____

_____

_____

_____

_____

_____

_____

List three reasons or items why you are grateful for your intuition today:

_____

_____

_____

_____

_____

_____

_____

_____

_____

Day 6

"Knowledge has three degrees- opinion, science, illumination.
The means or instrument of the first is sense; of the second, di-
alectic; of the the third, intuition."

-- Plotinus

List briefly the decisions and choices you made from your intuition:

_____

_____

_____

_____

_____

_____

_____

_____

_____

_____

_____

_____

_____

_____

_____

_____

_____

_____

_____

_____

How did it feel to make the choices/decisions from intuition?

_____

_____

_____

_____

_____

_____

_____

_____

_____

_____

_____

_____

_____

_____

_____

_____

_____

_____

_____

_____

_____

_____

_____

_____

_____

_____

What new insights or concepts will you take forward into the next day based on your experiences?

_____

_____

_____

_____

_____

_____

_____

_____

_____

_____

List three reasons or items why you are grateful for your intuition today:

_____

_____

_____

_____

_____

_____

_____

_____

_____

_____

Day 7

"You will do foolish things, but do them with enthusiasm."
-- Colette

List briefly the decisions and choices you made from your intuition:

_____

_____

_____

_____

_____

_____

_____

_____

_____

_____

_____

_____

_____

_____

_____

_____

_____

_____

_____

_____

_____

_____

_____

_____

_____

_____

How did it feel to make the choices/decisions from intuition?

_____

_____

_____

_____

_____

_____

_____

_____

_____

_____

_____

_____

_____

_____

_____

_____

_____

_____

_____

_____

_____

_____

What new insights or concepts will you take forward into the next day based on your experiences?

_____
_____
_____
_____
_____
_____
_____
_____
_____
_____

List three reasons or items why you are grateful for your intuition today:

_____
_____
_____
_____
_____
_____
_____
_____
_____
_____

"The outward freedom that we shall attain will only be in exact proportion to the inward freedom to which we may have grown at a given moment. And if this is a correct view of freedom, our chief energy must be concentrated on achieving reform -- from within. "

-- Gandhi

Intuition Insights Commitments

What pieces of these exercises were the most powerful for you?

_____

_____

_____

_____

_____

_____

_____

_____

_____

_____

What practice or focus gave you the most energy?

_____

_____

_____

_____

_____

_____

_____

_____

_____

_____

_____

What commitments would you like to make to yourself to ensure you continue to understand your intuition?

_____

_____

_____

_____

_____

_____

_____

_____

_____

_____

_____

_____

_____

_____

_____

_____

_____

_____

_____

_____

_____

_____

_____

Intuition of a Leader

Use this piece as a guide, a remembrance about what it is to take a risk, which is strong and centered. So much in our society says to gather the facts before making a decision; yet in truth and reality the greater percentage of decisions are made from the gut, from feeling.

Now I can just hear my scientists and logicians saying, "how can this be true" when so much of their lives are spent in pure and empirical facts. Yet, begin to really look how great ideas begin and how they start … often from a notion, an idea, a concept etc. Then data and research are found to support the idea. The concepts are the beginning and the facts are the result of a creative reorganization of old thoughts.

Ultimately what sets leaders apart from others is the ability to listen to their hearts, trust their intuition and take the risk to follow both.

What feeds into the final decision has little to do with fact and more to do with feeling. To know one's feelings, own senses, and body helps to ensure when taking a risk, it is coming from one's truth, heart, and center.

"What your heart thinks is great, is great.
The soul's emphasis is always right."
--Ralph Waldo Emerson

"As soon as you trust yourself you will know how to live."
-- Johann Wolfgang von Goethe

How did this look into myself support my sense of centeredness?

_____

_____

_____

_____

_____

_____

_____

_____

_____

_____

_____

_____

_____

_____

_____

_____

_____

_____

_____

_____

_____

What do I have a taste or interest for now?

_____

_____

_____

_____

_____

_____

_____

_____

_____

_____

_____

_____

_____

_____

_____

_____

_____

_____

_____

_____

_____

_____

_____

_____

_____

_____

_____

_____

What feels like the right next step for me?

_____

_____

_____

_____

_____

_____

_____

_____

_____

_____

_____

_____

_____

_____

_____

_____

_____

_____

_____

_____

_____

_____

_____

_____

"Begin today....
listen to your voice and live your truth
in a way which honors you and others."
~Bobbie Goheen

www.ingramcontent.com/pod-product-compliance
Lightning Source LLC
Chambersburg PA
CBHW022120170526
45157CB00004B/1704